©1996 Grandreams Ltd

Published by Grandreams Ltd,
Jadwin House,
205-211 Kentish Town Road,
London, NW5 2JU.

Written by Richard Neilson.

Designed by Joanna Davies, Sue Bartram and Louise Ivimy.

Printed in Italy.

All information believed correct at time of going to press. This is an unofficial publication and has no connection with the organising bodies of the European Championship, nor with any of the national squads involved. The publishers regret they cannot enter into correspondence regarding text or photographs in this book.

CONTENTS

- ENGLAND EXPECTS! 6
- THE VENUES 8
- ENGLAND'S SUPERSTARS 10
- SCOTLAND 16
- BULGARIA 20
- CROATIA 21
- CZECH REPUBLIC 22
- DENMARK 23
- CHAMPIONSHIP CHART 24
- FRANCE 26
- GERMANY 28
- HOLLAND 30
- ITALY 32
- PORTUGAL 34
- ROMANIA 35
- RUSSIA 36
- SPAIN 37
- SWITZERLAND 38
- TURKEY 39
- THE STORY OF THE EUROPEAN CHAMPIONSHIP 40

ENGLAND EXPECTS!

THE 1996 EUROPEAN CHAMPIONSHIP WILL BE THE FIRST MAJOR INTERNATIONAL SOCCER TOURNAMENT TO BE STAGED IN ENGLAND FOR THIRTY YEARS...

Terry Venables, the man who hopes to take England to the top this summer...

The last time around – in 1966 the story ended in triumph for the host nation. Under the determined management of Alf Ramsey (later 'Sir Alf') and the inspirational captaincy of Bobby Moore, England won football's top honour - the World Cup itself!

In a famous final at Wembley, Ramsey's team beat West Germany 4-2. It was a dramatic game that went into extra time and included one of the most talked-about goals in soccer history.

That sunny afternoon at Wembley should have marked the beginning of great things for English international football. Since then, however, the national side, under the guidance of a succession of managers - Joe Mercer (briefly), Don Revie, Ron Greenwood, Bobby Robson and Graham Taylor – have tried to emulate Sir Alf's feat of that Golden Summer of '66, but without success.

Two years after the World Cup triumph England finished third in the European Championship and they were among the favourites to win the World Cup again in 1970, but were eliminated at the quarter-finals stage.

Bobby Robson came closest when he led England to fourth place in the 1990 World Cup finals in Italy. That was the tournament in which the young Paul Gascoigne shed a tear or two and became, for a while, the hottest property in the game.

...And this is what he hopes to win the European Championship trophy

Apart from that it has largely been a question of hope and frustration for England's long-suffering fans.

Let's hope that the summer of 1996 will bring that long-awaited change of fortunes for English football, under the leadership of Terry Venables...

THE VENUES

THESE ARE THE GREAT GROUNDS CHOSEN TO STAGE THE 1996 EUROPEAN CHAMPIONSHIP...

GROUP A

WEMBLEY STADIUM

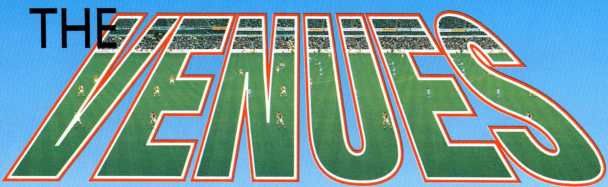

The Opening Ceremony, all of England's Group A ties, one quarter-final, a semi-final and the final itself will be played on Wembley's famous turf!

VILLA PARK

The home of Aston Villa has always been one of England's finest football grounds. This summer the famous old stadium will share the Group A fixtures with Wembley and will host one of the quarter-final games.

GROUP B

ELLAND ROAD

Leeds United's superb stadium will stage three Group B games...

ST. JAMES' PARK

Sharing Group B duties, with three games, will be St. James' Park, home of Newcastle United

OLD TRAFFORD

Manchester United's famous stadium, with its increased capacity, will stage three Group C games, a quarter-final and a semi-final.

ANFIELD

The home of Liverpool FC will see three opening group games, plus one of the quarter-final matches.

HILLSBOROUGH and THE CITY GROUND

Group D matches will be shared between Sheffield Wednesday's Hillsborough (left) and Nottingham Forest's City Ground.

ENGLAND'S

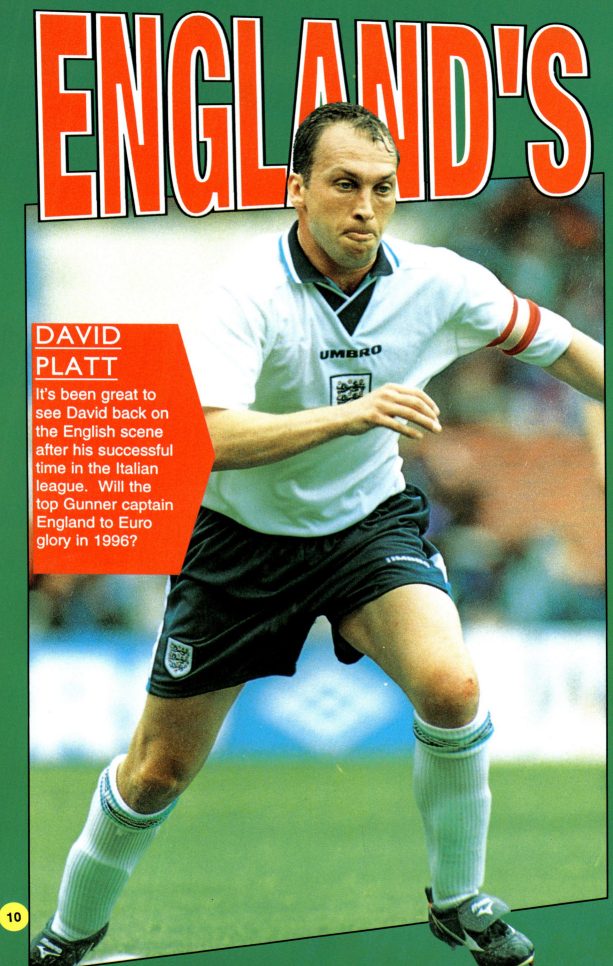

DAVID PLATT

It's been great to see David back on the English scene after his successful time in the Italian league. Will the top Gunner captain England to Euro glory in 1996?

SUPERSTARS

England's boss Terry Venables has some great talent to choose from. Here are just some of the stars who will be striving to be in Terry's squad this summer...

PAUL GASCOIGNE
Now a superstar north of the border with Rangers. The European Championship could provide Paul with just the stage on which to repeat his brilliant form in the World Cup six years ago!

ALAN SHEARER

Despite the fact that Blackburn found themselves struggling in the opening months of 1995/96, super striker Alan Shearer maintained his consistency by banging in goal after goal. This summer he'll be attempting to do the same in England's quest for the European Championship.

NICKY BARMBY

Nicky has become a great favourite at Middlesbrough's Riverside Stadium. He is a terrific midfielder with the knack of scoring spectacular goals and he looks like being an England regular for many years to come.

TIM FLOWERS

One of the most consistent and reliable keepers around, Tim vies for England's No.1 jersey with David Seaman.

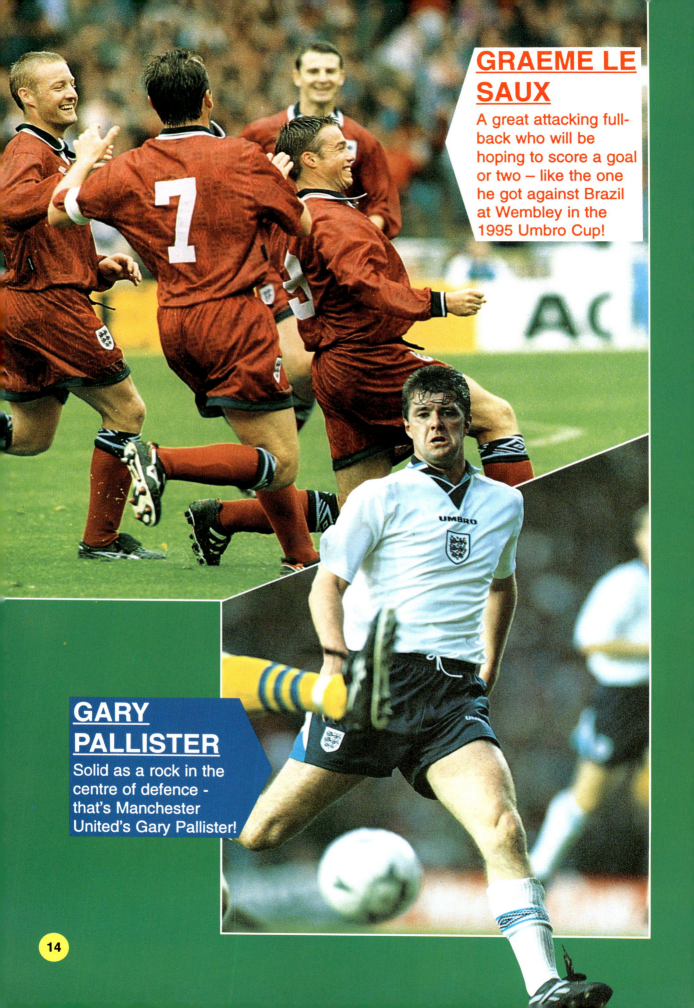

GRAEME LE SAUX

A great attacking full-back who will be hoping to score a goal or two – like the one he got against Brazil at Wembley in the 1995 Umbro Cup!

GARY PALLISTER

Solid as a rock in the centre of defence - that's Manchester United's Gary Pallister!

STEVE McMANAMAN

Liverpool's midfield ace is among the most consistently creative players in the country. His inclusion must be high on Terry Venables' list of priorities.

WARREN BARTON

The Newcastle defender is one of the best right-sided defenders in Europe.

COMPLETE THIS CHART WHEN THE ENGLAND SQUAD IS ANNOUNCED

1. _____
2. _____
3. _____
4. _____
5. _____
6. _____
7. _____
8. _____
9. _____
10. _____
11. _____
12. _____
13. _____
14. _____
15. _____
16. _____
17. _____
18. _____
19. _____
20. _____
21. _____
22. _____

SCOTLAND

Scott Booth in action

SCOTLAND FACT FILE

GOVERNING BODY: Scottish Football Association, Glasgow
FOUNDED: 1873
NATIONAL COLOURS: Dark blue shirts, white shorts, red socks
MANAGER/COACH: Craig Brown
PREVIOUS BEST IN EUROPEAN CHAMPIONSHIP:
First Round in 1992

Scotland qualified for the 1996 European Championship finals by finishing second, behind Russia, in Group 8. Their last match in the group was a splendid 5-0 victory over San Marino. Having learned that they were sure of qualification earlier on the day of the match, the Scots were able to relax, and they really turned on the style. Goals from Eoin Jess, Scott Booth, Ally McCoist and Pat Nevin, plus an unfortunate own goal by Fabio Francini, sent the Hampden Park crowd home happy.

Before that Scotland had recorded some other impressive qualifying results, including away wins in Finland, San Marino and the Faroe Islands and two all-important draws against Group winners Russia.

Manager Craig Brown declared himself delighted with qualification and the way in which it had been achieved by his squad. And he had good reason to be pleased with himself – Brown is the first Scottish manager to achieve European Championship qualification at the first attempt.

His super squad includes

THE ROAD TO ENGLAND
QUALIFYING GROUP EIGHT

Finland	0	**Scotland**	2
Faroes	1	Greece	5
Scotland	5	**Faroes**	1
Greece	4	Finland	0
Russia	4	San Marino	0
Scotland	1	**Russia**	1
Greece	2	San Marino	0
Finland	5	Faroes	0
Finland	4	San Marino	1
Greece	1	**Scotland**	0
Russia	0	**Scotland**	0
San Marino	0	Finland	2
San Marino	0	**Scotland**	2
Greece	0	Russia	3
Faroes	0	Finland	4
Russia	3	Faroes	0
Faroes	3	San Marino	0
Faroes	0	**Scotland**	2
San Marino	0	Russia	7
Finland	2	Greece	1
Scotland	1	**Greece**	0
Finland	0	Russia	6
Scotland	1	**Finland**	0
Faroes	2	Russia	5
San Marino	0	Greece	4
Russia	2	Greece	1
San Marino	1	Faroes	3
Scotland	5	**San Marino**	0
Russia	3	Finland	1
Greece	5	Faroes	0

	P	W	D	L	F	A	Pts
Russia	10	8	2	0	34	5	26
Scotland	**10**	**7**	**2**	**1**	**19**	**3**	**23**
Greece	10	6	0	4	23	9	18
Finland	10	5	0	5	18	18	15
Faroes	10	2	0	8	10	35	6
San Marino	10	0	0	10	2	36	0

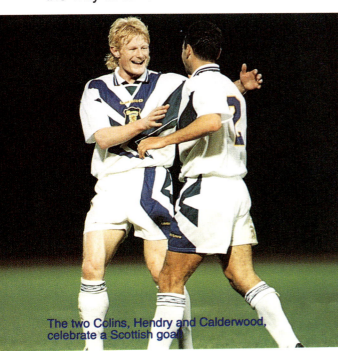

The two Colins, Hendry and Calderwood, celebrate a Scottish goal

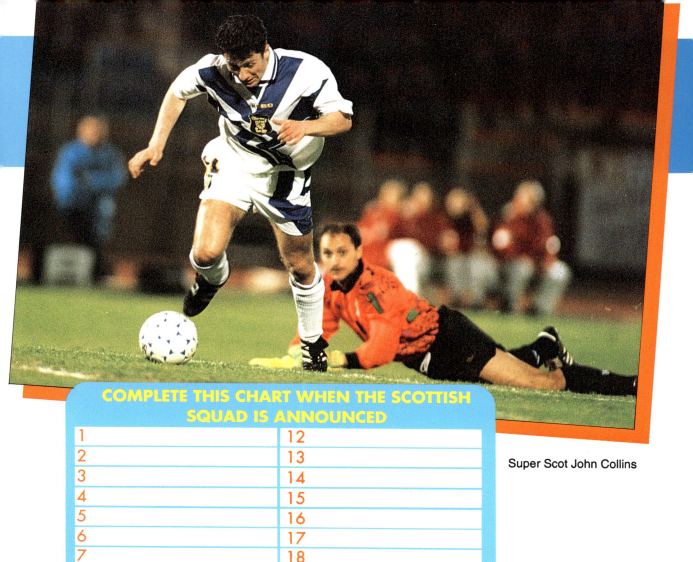

Super Scot John Collins

COMPLETE THIS CHART WHEN THE SCOTTISH SQUAD IS ANNOUNCED

1	12
2	13
3	14
4	15
5	16
6	17
7	18
8	19
9	20
10	21
11	22

inspirational skipper and midfield maestro Gary McAllister, striker supreme Ally McCoist, defensive rock Colin Hendry, wily winger Pat Nevin, the exciting Eion Jess and a whole host of other talents. These are just some of the guys who will be battling to bring home Scotland's first major international honour.

It's great to see Scotland among the contenders. The presence of the blue-and-white army in England will add an extra touch of spice to the occasion.

After all, there are many fans north and south of the border who still miss those annual matches between the two countries. And there are even those who call for a return of the old Home Internationals tournament that was once an integral part of the British soccer scene.

The Scotland v England game was the oldest international fixture of them all. It began way back in 1872 with a 0-0 draw in Glasgow, and it went on as a regular fixture until the Home International tournament was abandoned in 1983-84. Of the 107 Scotland v England encounters

England won 43, Scotland won 40 and 24 were drawn; England scored 188 goals, Scotland 168 goals. The last time the two countries met was in the Rous Cup in May 1989 when England won 2-0 at Hampden Park with goals from Chris Waddle and Steve Bull.

It will be great when the two countries meet again at Wembley on 15 June 1996.

Colin Hendry - a rock in Scotland's defence

Scottish skipper Gary McAllister – will he carry the Cup back to Glasgow?

BULGARIA

Bulgaria has been a threatening presence on the international soccer scene for many years. In the 1994 World Cup finals in America they finished in fourth place, having lost to Italy in the semi-finals. Along the way they had beaten Argentina and Greece in the opening round and eliminated mighty Germany 2-1 in the quarter-finals.

Now Bulgaria has qualified for the European Championship from Group 7 – the same group as Germany.

For a while Bulgaria led the table and were looking the superior side in the group – it was only a last game defeat by Germany that reversed the situation.

The Bulgarian squad, under the management of Dimitar Penev, boast some of Europe's top stars including super strikers Hristo Stoichkov (who plays for Parma in Italy) and Emil Kostadinov (who plays for Bayern Munich in Germany).

THE ROAD TO ENGLAND QUALIFYING GROUP SEVEN

Wales	2	Albania	0
Georgia	0	Moldova	1
Moldova	3	Wales	2
Bulgaria	**2**	**Georgia**	**0**
Albania	1	Germany	2
Georgia	5	Wales	0
Bulgaria	**4**	**Moldova**	**1**
Wales	**0**	**Bulgaria**	**3**
Moldova	0	Germany	3
Albania	0	Georgia	1
Germany	2	Albania	1
Georgia	0	Germany	2
Bulgaria	**3**	**Wales**	**1**
Albania	3	Moldova	0
Germany	1	Wales	1
Moldova	**0**	**Bulgaria**	**3**
Georgia	2	Albania	0
Bulgaria	**3**	**Germany**	**2**
Wales	0	Georgia	1
Moldova	2	Albania	3
Germany	4	Georgia	1
Wales	1	Moldova	0
Albania	**1**	**Bulgaria**	**1**
Bulgaria	**3**	**Albania**	**0**
Germany	6	Moldova	1
Wales	1	Germany	2
Georgia	**2**	**Bulgaria**	**1**
Germany	**3**	**Bulgaria**	**1**
Albania	1	Wales	1
Moldova	3	Georgia	2

	P	W	D	L	F	A	Pts
Germany	10	8	1	1	27	10	25
Bulgaria	**10**	**7**	**1**	**2**	**24**	**10**	**22**
Georgia	10	5	0	5	14	13	15
Moldova	10	3	0	7	11	27	9
Wales	10	2	2	6	9	19	8
Albania	10	2	2	6	10	16	8

BULGARIA FACT FILE

GOVERNING BODY: Bulgarian Football Union, Sofia
FOUNDED: 1923
NATIONAL COLOURS: White Shirts, green shorts, red socks
MANAGER/COACH: Dimitar Penev
PREVIOUS BEST IN EUROPEAN CHAMPIONSHIP: Quarter-finalists in 1968

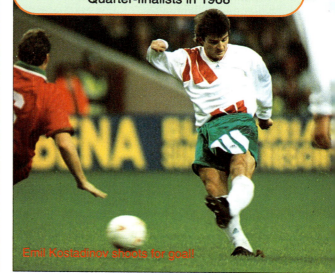

Emil Kostadinov shoots for goal

CROATIA

The Croatian national team was scheduled to play England at Wembley last September – but the match was cancelled and England took on Colombia instead. While we obviously enjoyed the visit of the South Americans (especially keeper Higuita's fabulous 'Scorpion' kick), we were denied the chance of assessing the Croats at close quarters – which would have been of more practical help to Terry Venables and Co.

Since Croatia declared her independence from the former Yugoslavia in 1991, they have emerged through the European Championship qualifying round as a real threat to the rest of the Continent.

Perhaps this should not sound so surprising, as many members of Croatia's talented squad were in the Yugoslavian team that won the World Youth Cup back in 1987. And if political events had not over taken the region in the way they did, then who knows what Yugoslavia might have achieved in Sweden in 1992?

On the way to this year's finals – in Qualifying Group 4 – Croatia were quite magnificent, beating everyone else in the group, including a 2-1 away victory in Italy. They finished top, level on points with Italy but with a superior goal difference.

Now, the distinctive red and white chequered shirts of Croatia could become a familiar sight all the way through the finals!

CROATIA FACT FILE

GOVERNING BODY: Croatian Football Federation, Zagreb
FOUNDED: 1991
NATIONAL COLOURS: Red/white chequered shirts, white shorts, blue socks
MANAGER/COACH: Otto Baric

THE ROAD TO ENGLAND QUALIFYING GROUP FOUR

Estonia	0	**Croatia**	2
Slovenia	1	Italy	1
Ukraine	0	Lithuania	2
Estonia	0	Italy	2
Croatia	2	**Lithuania**	0
Ukraine	0	Slovenia	0
Ukraine	3	Estonia	0
Slovenia	1	Lithuania	2
Italy	1	**Croatia**	2
Italy	4	Estonia	1
Croatia	4	**Ukraine**	0
Slovenia	3	Estonia	0
Ukraine	0	Italy	2
Lithuania	0	**Croatia**	0
Lithuania	0	Italy	1
Croatia	2	**Slovenia**	0
Estonia	0	Ukraine	1
Lithuania	2	Slovenia	1
Estonia	1	Slovenia	3
Ukraine	1	**Croatia**	0
Estonia	0	Lithuania	1
Croatia	7	**Estonia**	1
Italy	1	Slovenia	0
Lithuania	1	Ukraine	3
Croatia	1	**Italy**	1
Slovenia	3	Ukraine	2
Lithuania	5	Estonia	0
Italy	3	Ukraine	1
Slovenia	1	**Croatia**	2
Italy	4	Lithuania	0

	P	W	D	L	F	A	Pts
Croatia	10	7	2	1	22	5	23
Italy	10	7	2	1	20	6	23
Lithuania	10	5	1	4	13	12	16
Ukraine	10	4	1	5	11	15	13
Slovenia	10	3	2	5	13	13	11
Estonia	10	0	0	10	3	3	10

Action from the Croatia v Italy qualifying match

CZECH REPUBLIC

THE ROAD TO ENGLAND
QUALIFYING GROUP FIVE

Czech Rep	6	Malta	1
Luxembourg	0	Holland	4
Norway	1	Byelorussia	0
Malta	0	Czech Rep	0
Byelorussia	2	Luxembourg	0
Norway	1	Holland	1
Byelorussia	0	Norway	4
Holland	0	Czech Rep	0
Malta	0	Norway	1
Holland	5	Luxembourg	0
Malta	0	Luxembourg	1
Czech Rep	4	Byelorussia	2
Luxembourg	0	Norway	2
Holland	4	Malta	0
Byelorussia	1	Malta	1
Czech Rep	3	Holland	1
Norway	5	Luxembourg	0
Byelorussia	1	Holland	0
Luxembourg	1	Czech Rep	0
Norway	2	Malta	0
Norway	1	Czech Rep	1
Czech Rep	2	Norway	0
Luxembourg	1	Malta	0
Holland	1	Byelorussia	0
Byelorussia	0	Czech Rep	2
Malta	0	Holland	4
Luxembourg	0	Byelorussia	0
Malta	0	Byelorussia	2
Czech Rep	3	Luxembourg	0
Holland	3	Norway	0

	P	W	D	L	F	A	Pts
Czech Rep	10	6	3	1	21	6	21
Holland	10	6	2	2	23	5	20
Norway	10	6	2	2	17	7	20
Byelorussia	10	3	2	5	8	13	11
Luxembourg	10	3	1	6	3	21	10
Malta	10	0	2	8	2	22	2

CZECH REPUBLIC FACT FILE

GOVERNING BODY: Football Association of Czech Republic, Prague
NATIONAL COLOURS: Red shirts, white shorts, blue socks
MANAGER/COACH: Dusan Uhrin
PREVIOUS BEST IN EUROPEAN CHAMPIONSHIP: Champions in 1976 (as Czechoslovakia)

The Czech Republic topped the closest-run of all the qualifying groups – Group 5. Before the last games were played it was still a three horse race, with Norway sitting on top of the table with 20 points, followed by the Czech Republic (18) and Holland (17).

Then the Czech Republic beat Luxembourg 3-0 in Prague with goals from Berger and Drulack, who scored twice. This ensured their qualification with 21 points, and left Holland and Norway to decide the final group placings. (Holland won that match in Rotterdam 3-0, to finish second on 20 points and with a better goal difference than Norway, who were eliminated).

One of the best Czech results earlier in their campaign was a brilliant 3-1 victory over Holland in Prague, in April 1995, with goals from from Skhuravy, Nemecek and Berger. The worst Czech result, however, was a 1-0 defeat by Luxembourg two months later. It was this result along with a point dropped in Malta which held up the Republic's progress and led to that nail-biting finish in Group 5.

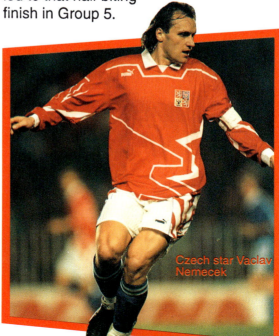

Czech star Vaclav Nemecek

DENMARK

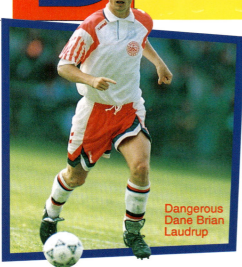

Dangerous Dane Brian Laudrup

THE ROAD TO ENGLAND QUALIFYING GROUP TWO

Cyprus	1	Spain	2
Macedonia	**1**	**Denmark**	**1**
Belgium	2	Armenia	0
Armenia	0	Cyprus	0
Denmark	**3**	**Belgium**	**1**
Macedonia	0	Spain	2
Belgium	1	Macedonia	1
Spain	**3**	**Denmark**	**0**
Cyprus	2	Armenia	0
Belgium	1	Spain	4
Macedonia	3	Cyprus	0
Spain	1	Belgium	1
Cyprus	**1**	**Denmark**	**1**
Armenia	0	Spain	2
Belgium	2	Cyprus	0
Denmark	**1**	**Macedonia**	**0**
Armenia	2	Macedonia	2
Denmark	**4**	**Cyprus**	**0**
Mecedonia	0	Belgium	5
Spain	1	Armenia	0
Armenia	**0**	**Denmark**	**2**
Belgium	**1**	**Denmark**	**3**
Spain	6	Cyprus	0
Macedonia	1	Armenia	2
Armenia	0	Belgium	2
Denmark	**1**	**Spain**	**1**
Cyprus	1	Macedonia	1
Spain	3	Macedonia	0
Cyprus	1	Belgium	1
Denmark	**3**	**Armenia**	**1**

	P	W	D	L	F	A	Pts
Spain	10	8	2	0	25	4	26
Denmark	**10**	**6**	**3**	**1**	**19**	**9**	**21**
Belgium	10	4	3	3	17	13	15
Macedonia	10	1	4	5	9	18	7
Cyprus	10	1	4	5	6	20	7
Armenia	10	1	2	7	5	17	5

In the 1992 European Championship Denmark wrote their own special chapter in the folklore of the tournament. They arrived in Sweden as a late replacement for Yugoslavia who were banned from entry due to political unrest and sanctions imposed by UEFA. No one gave the Danes a hope of even doing well; they really were considered as makeweights, and were expected to make a swift return home.

But the Danes had other plans and, against all the odds, they became Champions of Europe – thanks to a display of sheer determination and a never-say-die attitude towards the task in hand.

Now Denmark have qualified for the 1996 finals in England, by finishing as Qualifying Group 2 runners-up behind Spain.

The big question on everyone's lips is: Can the Danes repeat their Golden Summer of '92? That would certainly be a high note for coach Richard Moller Nielsen to end his brilliant association with the national side.

Write them off at your peril!

DENMARK FACT FILE

GOVERNING BODY: Dansk Boldspil Union, Copenhagen
FOUNDED: 1889
NATIONAL COLOURS: Red shirts, white shorts, red socks
MANAGER/COACH: Richard Moller Nielsen
PREVIOUS BEST IN EUROPEAN CHAMPIONSHIP: Champions in 1992

EUROPEAN CHAM...
Use this chart to record the progres...

FIRST ROUND

GROUP A

DATE	VENUE	MATCH	RESULT
8 June	Wembley	ENGLAND V SWITZERLAND	____
10 June	Villa Park	HOLLAND V SCOTLAND	____
13 June	Villa Park	SWITZERLAND V HOLLAND	____
15 June	Wembley	SCOTLAND V ENGLAND	____
18 June	Villa Park	SCOTLAND V SWITZERLAND	____
18 June	Wembley	HOLLAND V ENGLAND	____

GROUP B

DATE	VENUE	MATCH	RESULT
9 June	Elland Road	SPAIN V BULGARIA	____
10 June	St James'	ROMANIA V FRANCE	____
13 June	St James'	BULGARIA V ROMANIA	____
15 June	Elland Road	FRANCE V SPAIN	____
18 June	St James'	FRANCE V BULGARIA	____
18 June	Elland Road	ROMANIA V SPAIN	____

GROUP C

DATE	VENUE	MATCH	RESULT
9 June	Old Trafford	GERMANY V CZECH REPUBLIC	____
11 June	Anfield	ITALY V RUSSIA	____
14 June	Anfield	CZECH REPUBLIC V ITALY	____
16 June	Old Trafford	RUSSIA V GERMANY	____
19 June	Anfield	RUSSIA V CZECH REPUBLIC	____
19 June	Old Trafford	ITALY V GERMANY	____

GROUP D

DATE	VENUE	MATCH	RESULT
9 June	Hillsborough	DENMARK V PORTUGAL	____
11 June	City Ground	TURKEY V CROATIA	____
14 June	City Ground	PORTUGAL V TURKEY	____
16 June	Hillsborough	CROATIA V DENMARK	____
19 June	City Ground	CROATIA V PORTUGAL	____
19 June	Hillsborough	TURKEY V DENMARK	____

QUARTER FINALS

DATE	VENUE	MATCH	RESULT
22 June	Anfield	WINNER GROUP B V RUNNER-UP GROUP A	____
22 June	Wembley	RUNNER-UP GROUP B V WINNER GROUP A	____
23 June	Old Trafford	WINNER GROUP C V RUNNER-UP GROUP D	____
23 June	Villa Park	RUNNER-UP GROUP C V WINNER GROUP D	____

24

PIONSHIP CHART
s of the tournament as it unfolds...

SEMI FINALS **FINAL**

DATE	VENUE	MATCH	RESULT
26 June	Old Trafford	ANFIELD WINNER V VILLA PARK WINNER	

DATE	VENUE	MATCH	RESULT
30 June	WEMBLEY	V	

DATE	VENUE	MATCH	RESULT
26 June	Wembley	WEMBLEY WINNER V OLD TRAFFORD WINNER	

FRANCE

Back in 1960 France finished fourth in the first-ever European Championship, behind the USSR, Yugoslavia and Czechoslovakia; in 1964 and '68 they were quarter-finalists. Between 1972 and 1980 came a period in the Euro doldrums as the French surprisingly failed to progress beyond the qualifying rounds.

Then came 1984 and the most glorious campaign in French football history, in which France not only hosted the finals, but dominated them completely. Inspired by the great Michel Platini – who scored in every round – they stormed to the final in Paris, where they beat Spain 2-0.

In an unexpected turn of events, France then failed to make it to the 1988 finals in West Germany, finishing

RIGHT: French midfield ace Youri Djorkaeff
LEFT: Didier Deschamps on the ball
ABOVE: Many French fans would love to see the return of Eric Cantona

third in their qualifying group behind the USSR and East Germany. They did make it, unbeaten, to Sweden in 1992, only to fall in the First Round (along with England) as Sweden and eventual Champions Denmark went through.

Now, France has once again qualified for the finals – as runners-up to Romania in Group 1 and as one of

THE ROAD TO ENGLAND
QUALIFYING GROUP ONE

Israel	2	Poland	1
Slovakia	**0**	**France**	**0**
Romania	3	Azerbaijan	0
France	**0**	**Romania**	**0**
Israel	2	Slovakia	2
Poland	1	Azerbaijan	0
Romania	3	Slovakia	2
Poland	**0**	**France**	**0**
Azerbaijan	0	Israel	2
Azerbaijan	**0**	**France**	**2**
Israel	1	Romania	1
Romania	2	Poland	1
Israel	**0**	**France**	**0**
Slovakia	4	Azerbaijan	1
Poland	4	Israel	3
France	**4**	**Slovakia**	**0**
Azerbaijan	1	Romania	4
Poland	5	Slovakia	0
Romania	2	Israel	1
France	**1**	**Poland**	**1**
Azerbaijan	0	Slovakia	1
France	**10**	**Azerbaijan**	**0**
Slovakia	1	Israel	0
Poland	0	Romania	0
Romania	**1**	**France**	**3**
Israel	2	Azerbaijan	0
Slovakia	4	Poland	1
Slovakia	0	Romania	2
Azerbaijan	0	Poland	0
France 2		**Israel**	**0**

	P	W	D	L	F	A	Pts
Romania	10	6	3	1	18	9	21
France	**10**	**5**	**5**	**0**	**22**	**2**	**20**
Slovakia	10	4	2	4	14	18	14
Poland	10	3	4	3	14	12	13
Israel	10	3	3	4	13	13	12
Azerbaijan	10	0	1	9	2	29	1

FRANCE FACT FILE
GOVERNING BODY:
Federation Francaise De Football, Paris
FOUNDED: 1918
NATIONAL COLOURS: Blue shirts, white shorts, red socks
MANAGER/COACH: Aimé Jacquet
PREVIOUS BEST IN EUROPEAN CHAMPIONSHIP:
Champions in 1984

only three sides to remain unbeaten en route to England (the others were Spain and Russia).

In fact, France's ten qualifiers were part of a remarkable seventeen match unbeaten run. All of which must put them among the front-runners this summer...

GERMANY

Germany really showed their class in their last qualifying match against Bulgaria in Group 7. Both countries had qualified by then and it was simply a question of who would finish first.

Germany won the match 3-1 to take their points tally to 25, the second highest in the qualifying tournament (only Russia and Spain amassed more points - 26 each). The German goals came from skipper Jurgen Klinsmann who scored twice (including one from the penalty spot) and Thomas Hassler – and the scintillating performance once again gave warning of Germany's intentions in this tournament.

They are, after all, the most successful European Championship country of them all, being the only one to win the title twice.

The first occasion was in 1972, when (as West Germany) they beat the USSR 3-0 in Brussels. The second was in Rome in 1980, when they beat Belgium 2-1. The Germans have also been runners-up twice, in 1976 and 1992.

But coach Berti Vogts and his squad of superstars won't be satisfied with second place again. They will be aiming for nothing less than that elusive third European Championship title!

Thomas Hassler moves forward

Matthias Sammer gets in a shot against Wales

Defender Markus Babbel challenges Ian Rush

Midfield ace Mario Basler

THE ROAD TO ENGLAND
QUALIFYING GROUP SEVEN

Wales	2	Albania	0
Georgia	0	Moldova	1
Moldova	3	Wales	2
Bulgaria	2	Georgia	0
Albania	**1**	**Germany**	**2**
Georgia	5	Wales	0
Bulgaria	4	Moldova	1
Wales	0	Bulgaria	3
Moldova	**0**	**Germany**	**3**
Albania	0	Georgia	1
Germany	**2**	**Albania**	**1**
Georgia	**0**	**Germany**	**2**
Bulgaria	3	Wales	1
Albania	3	Moldova	0
Germany	**1**	**Wales**	**1**
Moldova	0	Bulgaria	3
Georgia	2	Albania	0
Bulgaria	**3**	**Germany**	**2**
Wales	0	Georgia	1
Moldova	2	Albania	3
Germany	**4**	**Georgia**	**1**
Wales	1	Moldova	0
Albania	1	Bulgaria	1
Bulgaria	3	Albania	0
Germany	**6**	**Moldova**	**1**
Wales	**1**	**Germany**	**2**
Georgia	2	Bulgaria	1
Germany	**3**	**Bulgaria**	**1**
Albania	1	Wales	1
Moldova	3	Georgia	2

	P	W	D	L	F	A	Pts
Germany	**10**	**8**	**1**	**1**	**27**	**10**	**25**
Bulgaria	10	7	1	2	24	10	22
Georgia	10	5	0	5	14	13	15
Moldova	10	3	0	7	11	27	9
Wales	10	2	2	6	9	19	8
Albania	10	2	2	6	10	16	8

GERMANY FACT FILE

GOVERNING BODY: Deutsche Fussball-Bund, Frankfurt
Founded: 1900
NATIONAL COLOURS: White shirts, black shorts, white socks
MANAGER/COACH: Berti Vogts
PREVIOUS BEST IN EUROPEAN CHAMPIONSHIP:
Champions in 1972, 1980 (as West Germany)

HOLLAND

Patrick Kluivert challenges for the ball

Holland must be thankful that the legendary 'Luck of the Irish' finally ran out for Jack Charlton and his boys in green in the last-place play-off at Anfield. The Dutch side won 2-0 to secure their qualification for the 1996 finals in England.

Coach Guus Hiddink certainly has some great players to call upon to meet the challenge of the European Championship finals. After all, Holland boasts one of the best youth development systems in the world, and one of the best clubs – Ajax of Amsterdam, the 1995 European Cup winners.

Ajax currently supply the core of the Dutch national squad from goalkeeper Edwin Van der Sar through defenders Danny Blind, Frank De Boer and

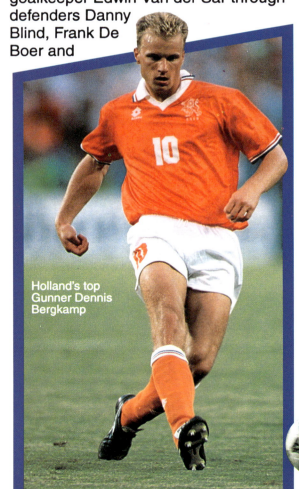

Holland's top Gunner Dennis Bergkamp

HOLLAND FACT FILE

GOVERNING BODY: Koninklijke Nederlandsche Voetbalbond
FOUNDED: 1889
NATIONAL COLOURS: Orange shirts, white shorts, orange socks
MANAGER/COACH: Guus Hiddink
PREVIOUS BEST IN EUROPEAN CHAMPIONSHIP: Champions 1988

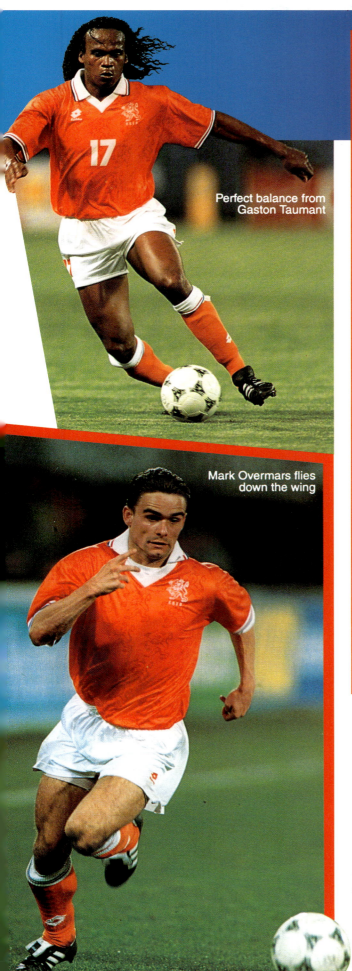

Perfect balance from Gaston Taumant

Mark Overmars flies down the wing

THE ROAD TO ENGLAND
QUALIFYING GROUP FIVE

Czech Rep	6	Malta	1
Luxembourg	**0**	**Holland**	**4**
Norway	1	Byelorussia	0
Malta	0	Czech Rep	0
Byelorussia	2	Luxembourg	0
Norway	**1**	**Holland**	**1**
Byelorussia	0	Norway	4
Holland	**0**	**Czech Rep**	**0**
Malta	0	Norway	1
Holland	**5**	**Luxembourg**	**0**
Malta	0	Luxembourg	1
Czech Rep	4	Byelorussia	2
Luxembourg	0	Norway	2
Holland	**4**	**Malta**	**0**
Byelorussia	1	Malta	1
Czech Rep	**3**	**Holland**	**1**
Norway	5	Luxembourg	0
Byelorussia	**1**	**Holland**	**0**
Luxembourg	1	Czech Rep	0
Norway	2	Malta	0
Norway	1	Czech Rep	1
Czech Rep	2	Norway	0
Luxembourg	1	Malta	0
Holland	**1**	**Byelorussia**	**0**
Byelorussia	0	Czech Rep	2
Malta	**0**	**Holland**	**4**
Luxembourg	0	Byelorussia	0
Malta	0	Byelorussia	2
Czech Rep	3	Luxembourg	0
Holland	**3**	**Norway**	**0**

	P	W	D	L	F	A	Pts
Czech Rep.	10	6	3	1	21	6	23
Holland	**10**	**6**	**2**	**2**	**23**	**5**	**20**
Norway	10	6	2	2	17	7	20
Byelorussia	10	3	2	5	8	13	11
Luxembourg	10	3	1	6	3	21	10
Malta	10	0	2	8	2	22	2

Play off: Holland beat Rep. of Ireland 2-0

Michael Reiziger, to midfield star Ronald De Boer and forwards Patrick Kluivert and Marc Overmars.

Then there are the foreign-based Dutchmen, like Dennis Bergkamp who plays for Arsenal in England, and Clarence Seedorf who plays for Sampdoria in Italy.

After the scare of the play-off situation, Holland will be anxious to capitalise on their second chance.

They are potential winners!

ITALY

Italy qualified for the finals as runners-up to Croatia in Group 4 – and then became favourites to finish the tournament as the 1996 European Champions.

If the Italians manage to live up to those expectations they will become only the second nation to win the Championship twice. They first lifted the title in 1968, when they hosted the tournament and beat Yugoslavia in a replayed final in Rome.

The Italian fans, who are among the most passionate in the world, are impatient for true success. They feel it's about time that their team won another major trophy – the last one came fourteen years ago when Italy won the 1982 World Cup, beating West Germany 3-1 in the final in Madrid.

Since then Italy has finished fourth in the 1980 European Championship (they also hosted the finals of that tournament); in the 1986 World Cup in Mexico Italy went out to France in the Second Round; in '88 they reached the semi-finals of the European Championship in Germany,

Italian keeper Gianluca Pagliuca gives his orders!

ITALY FACT FILE

GOVERNING BODY: Federazione Italiana Giuoco Calcio, Rome
FOUNDED: 1898
NATIONAL COLOURS: Blue shirts, white shorts, blue/white socks
MANAGER/COACH: Arrigo Sacchi
PREVIOUS BEST IN EUROPEAN CHAMPIONSHIP: Champions 1968

losing 2-0 to the USSR.

Then came the Italia '90 World Cup finals, a spectacular tournament in which Italian hopes ran very high. But once again they fell at the semi-finals stage, losing on penalties to Argentina. Their only consolation was third place, gained with a 2-1 win over England.

Gianfranco Zola in action in a friendly against Germany

THE ROAD TO ENGLAND QUALIFYING GROUP FOUR

Estonia	0	Croatia	2
Slovenia	**1**	**Italy**	**1**
Ukraine	0	Lithuania	2
Estonia	**0**	**Italy**	**2**
Croatia	2	Lithuania	0
Ukraine	0	Slovenia	0
Ukraine	3	Estonia	0
Slovenia	1	Lithuania	2
Italy	**1**	**Croatia**	**2**
Italy	**4**	**Estonia**	**1**
Croatia	4	Ukraine	0
Slovenia	3	Estonia	0
Ukraine	**0**	**Italy**	**2**
Lithuania	0	Croatia	0
Lithuania	**0**	**Italy**	**1**
Croatia	2	Slovenia	0
Estonia	0	Ukraine	1
Lithuania	2	Slovenia	1
Estonia	1	Slovenia	3
Ukraine	1	Croatia	0
Estonia	0	Lithuania	1
Croatia	7	Estonia	1
Italy	**1**	**Slovenia**	**0**
Lithuania	1	Ukraine	3
Croatia	**1**	**Italy**	**1**
Slovenia	3	Ukraine	2
Lithuania	5	Estonia	0
Italy	**3**	**Ukraine**	**1**
Slovenia	1	Croatia	2
Italy	**4**	**Lithuania**	**0**

	P	W	D	L	F	A	Pts
Croatia	10	7	2	1	22	5	23
Italy	**10**	**7**	**2**	**1**	**20**	**6**	**23**
Lithuania	10	5	1	4	13	12	16
Ukraine	10	4	1	5	11	15	13
Slovenia	10	3	2	5	13	13	11
Estonia	10	0	0	10	3	31	0

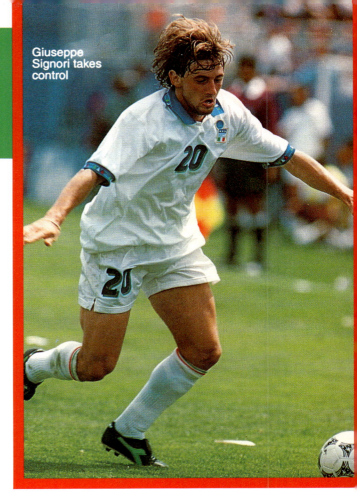

Giuseppe Signori takes control

Italy reached a low ebb in 1992, when they failed to reach the European Championship finals in Sweden. But they made up for things in the 1994 World Cup finals in America, in which they came so very close to glory. After a tense match in the final against Brazil, which remained in a 0-0 deadlock after extra time, the Championship of the world was decided on penalties. When Roberto Baggio's shot went over the bar Italy were resigned to runners-up spot.

Now Arrigo Sacchi and his squad of highly talented superstars – including Gianfranco Zola, Giuseppe Signori, Roberto Donadoni, Paolo Maldini and Gianluca Pagliuca – know that nothing less than the European title will satisfy those fans!

Roberto Donadoni in action

PORTUGAL

Portugal have emerged in recent years as one of Europe's top footballing nations. They headed the Group 6 qualifiers ahead of the Republic of Ireland (who went into the last-place play-off against Holland).

They really showed their class on a rain-soaked night in Lisbon when they destroyed the Irish challenge with a magnificent 3-0 victory. True, the Irish side was weakened by the absence of some key midfielders but that should not detract from the Portuguese performance. The goals all came in the second half, from Rui Costa, Helder and Cadete.

Portugal are one of those countries who feel they deserve a big honour. 1996 could be the year of the Portuguese!

The Portuguese team line-up for the camera before their qualifier against Ireland

THE ROAD TO ENGLAND QUALIFYING GROUP SIX

Northern Ireland	4	Liechtenstein	1
Liechtenstein	0	Austria	4
Northern Ireland	**1**	**Portugal**	**2**
Latvia	0	Rep Ireland	3
Latvia	**1**	**Portugal**	**3**
Austria	1	Northern Ireland	2
Rep Ireland	4	Liechtenstein	0
Portugal	**1**	**Austria**	**0**
Liechtenstein	0	Latvia	1
Northern Ireland	0	Rep Ireland	4
Portugal	**8**	**Liechtenstein**	**0**
Rep Ireland	1	Northern Ireland	1
Austria	5	Latvia	0
Rep Ireland	**1**	**Portugal**	**0**
Latvia	0	Northern Ireland	1
Austria	7	Liechtenstein	0
Portugal	**3**	**Latvia**	**2**
Liechtenstein	0	Rep Ireland	0
Northern Ireland	1	Latvia	2
Rep Ireland	1	Austria	3
Liechtenstein	**0**	**Portugal**	**7**
Latvia	3	Austria	2
Portugal	**1**	**Northern Ireland**	**1**
Austria	3	Rep Ireland	1
Latvia	1	Liechtenstein	0
Rep Ireland	2	Latvia	1
Austria	**1**	**Portugal**	**1**
Liechtenstein	0	Northern Ireland	4
Portugal	**3**	**Rep Ireland**	**0**
Northern Ireland	5	Austria	3

	P	W	D	L	F	A	Pts
Portugal	10	7	2	1	29	7	23
Rep Ireland	10	5	2	3	17	11	17
N Ireland	10	5	2	3	20	15	17
Austria	10	5	1	4	29	14	16
Latvia	10	4	0	6	11	20	12
Liechtenstein	10	0	1	9	1	40	1

PORTUGAL FACT FILE

GOVERNING BODY: Federacao Potuguesa De Futebol, Lisbon
FOUNDED: 1914
NATIONAL COLOURS: Red shirts, green shorts, red socks
MANAGER/COACH: Antonio Oliveira
PREVIOUS BEST IN EUROPEAN CHAMPIONSHIP: Semi-finalists in 1984

ROMANIA

Romania's 0-0 draw with Poland in Zabrze last September secured them a top two spot in Qualifying Group 1. A 3-1 defeat by France followed, leaving the Romanians the task of winning their last game away to Slovakia to finish top of the Group. They did so with relative ease, thanks to goals by Hagi and Munteanu, and confirmed their status as one of Europe's leading footballing nations.

Although Romania did not make it to the European Championship finals in Sweden in 1992, they did reach the final stages of the last two World Cups in '90 and '94. In Italy they got to the Second Round but went out to the Republic of Ireland on penalties. In the USA they reached the quarter-finals

ROMANIA FACT FILE
GOVERNING BODY:
Federatia Romana De Fotbal, Bucharest
FOUNDED: 1908
NATIONAL COLOURS: Yellow shirts, blue shorts, red socks
MANAGER/COACH: Anghel Iordanescu
PREVIOUS BEST IN EUROPEAN CHAMPIONSHIP: Quarter-finalists in 1960 and 1972

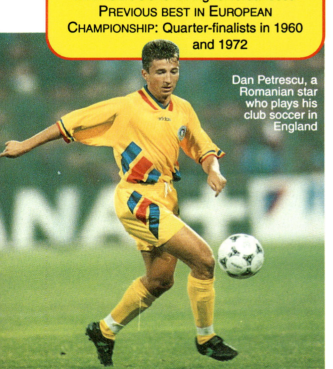

Dan Petrescu, a Romanian star who plays his club soccer in England

THE ROAD TO ENGLAND QUALIFYING GROUP ONE

Israel	2	Poland	1
Slovakia	0	France	0
Romania	**3**	**Azerbaijan**	**0**
France	**0**	**Romania**	**0**
Israel	2	Slovakia	2
Poland	1	Azerbaijan	0
Romania	**3**	**Slovakia**	**2**
Poland	0	France	0
Azerbaijan	0	Israel	2
Azerbaijan	0	France	2
Israel	**1**	**Romania**	**1**
Romania	**2**	**Poland**	**1**
Israel	0	France	0
Slovakia	4	Azerbaijan	1
Poland	4	Israel	3
France	4	Slovakia	0
Azerbaijan	**1**	**Romania**	**4**
Poland	5	Slovakia	0
Romania	**2**	**Israel**	**1**
France	1	Poland	1
Azerbaijan	0	Slovakia	1
France	10	Azerbaijan	0
Slovakia	1	Israel	0
Poland	**0**	**Romania**	**0**
Romania	**1**	**France**	**3**
Israel	2	Azerbaijan	0
Slovakia	4	Poland	1
Slovakia	**0**	**Romania**	**2**
Azerbaijan	0	Poland	0
France	2	Israel	0

	P	W	D	L	F	A	Pts
Romania	**10**	**6**	**3**	**1**	**18**	**9**	**21**
France	10	5	5	0	22	2	20
Slovakia	10	4	2	4	14	18	14
Poland	10	3	4	3	14	12	13
Israel	10	3	3	4	13	13	12
Azerbaijan	10	0	1	9	2	29	1

and again went out after a frustrating penalty shoot-out, this time against Sweden.

This year Iordanescu's Romania will definitely be one of the most entertaining and polished teams competing for the European title.

RUSSIA

Along with Spain, Russia were the first to qualify for the 1996 European Championship finals in England. And, like Spain, they won through with 26 points from a possible 30 – the highest total in the entire qualifying competition. Along the way they scored 34 goals, that's more than any other country in the whole qualifying competition.

Seven of those goals came in an away thrashing of San Marino, another six were notched against Finland in Helsinki. All of which means that Russia must be among the favourites to win the Championship in England this summer.

Among the stars at the disposal of Russian coach Oleg Romantsev are several who play in clubs around Europe – including Chelsea goalkeeper Dimitri Kharine and Everton's wing wonder Andrei Kanchelskis.

We all know how good they are...

Dimitri Kharine and Andrei Kanchelskis (above) – Russian aces who play in England

RUSSIA FACT FILE
GOVERNING BODY: Football Union of Russia, Moscow
FOUNDED: 1992
NATIONAL COLOURS: Red shirts, white shorts
MANAGER/COACH: Oleg Romantsev
PREVIOUS BEST IN EUROPEAN CHAMPIONSHIP: Champions in 1960 (as USSR)

THE ROAD TO ENGLAND
QUALIFYING GROUP EIGHT

Finland	0	Scotland	2
Faroes	1	Greece	5
Scotland	5	Faroes	1
Greece	4	Finland	0
Russia	**4**	**San Marino**	**0**
Scotland	1	Russia	1
Greece	2	San Marino	0
Finland	5	Faroes	0
Finland	4	San Marino	1
Greece	1	Scotland	0
Russia	**0**	**Scotland**	**0**
San Marino	0	Finland	2
San Marino	0	Scotland	2
Greece	**0**	**Russia**	**3**
Faroes	0	Finland	4
Russia	**3**	**Faroes**	**0**
Faroes	3	San Marino	0
Faroes	0	Scotland	2
San Marino	**0**	**Russia**	**7**
Finland	2	Greece	1
Scotland	1	Greece	0
Finland	**0**	**Russia**	**6**
Scotland	1	Finland	0
Faroes	**2**	**Russia**	**5**
San Marino	0	Greece	4
Russia	**2**	**Greece**	**1**
San Marino	1	Faroes	3
Scotland	5	San Marino	0
Russia	**3**	**Finland**	**1**
Greece	5	Faroes	0

	P	W	D	L	F	A	Pts
Russia	10	8	2	0	34	5	26
Scotland	10	7	2	1	19	3	23
Greece	10	6	0	4	23	9	18
Finland	10	5	0	5	18	18	15
Faroes	10	2	0	8	10	35	6
San Marino	10	0	0	10	2	36	0

SPAIN

Jose Maria Bakero watches the ball!

SPAIN FACT FILE
Governing Body: Real Federacion Espanol De Futbol, Madrid
Founded: 1913
National Colours: Red shirts, dark blue shorts, black socks with yellow trim
Manager/Coach: Javier Clemente
Previous best in European Championship: Champions in 1964

Spain made up for their absence in the 1992 European Championship finals by securing a place in England '96 with one qualifying match still remaining. Along with Russia they were the first to qualify. And, like Russia they amassed 26 points along the way.

This success is great news for team boss Javier Clemente, a former Athletic Bilbao player and manager, who took over the top job in 1992 after Spain's failure to make it to Sweden. That setback came as a real shock to Spanish fans and players alike – it was the first time their country had not reached a major international finals since the mid-70s.

The Spanish squad has qualified thanks to a mixture of sheer talent and dogged determination. Under Clemente's leadership they have proved an extremely difficult outfit to break down. Solid defence work and a skilful midfield have been dominant factors. En route to England they chalked up some impressive results in Qualifying Group 2, including a 4-1 away win against Belgium and a 6-0 drubbing of Cyprus in Granada.

Among the Spanish stars to look out for this summer will be Caminero in midfield, the veteran goalkeeper Zubizarretta, the tough central defender Fernando Hierro, midfield marvels Luis Enrique and Donato and striker Julen Guerrero...

Dramatic expression from Andoni Goikoetxea

THE ROAD TO ENGLAND
QUALIFYING GROUP TWO

Cyprus	1	Spain	2
Macedonia	1	Denmark	1
Belgium	2	Armenia	0
Armenia	0	Cyprus	0
Denmark	3	Belgium	1
Macedonia	0	Spain	2
Belgium	1	Macedonia	1
Spain	3	Denmark	0
Cyprus	2	Armenia	0
Belgium	1	Spain	4
Macedonia	3	Cyprus	0
Spain	1	Belgium	1
Cyprus	1	Denmark	1
Armenia	0	Spain	2
Belgium	2	Cyprus	0
Denmark	1	Macedonia	0
Armenia	2	Macedonia	2
Denmark	4	Cyprus	0
Macedonia	0	Belgium	5
Spain	1	Armenia	0
Armenia	0	Denmark	2
Belgium	1	Denmark	3
Spain	6	Cyprus	0
Macedonia	1	Armenia	2
Armenia	0	Belgium	2
Denmark	1	Spain	1
Cyprus	1	Macedonia	1
Spain	3	Macedonia	0
Cyprus	1	Belgium	1
Denmark	3	Armenia	1

	P	W	D	L	F	A	Pts
Spain	10	8	2	0	25	4	26
Denmark	10	6	3	1	19	9	21
Belgium	10	4	3	3	17	13	15
Macedonia	10	1	4	5	9	18	7
Cyprus	10	1	4	5	6	20	7
Armenia	10	1	2	7	5	17	5

SWITZERLAND

It took a quietly spoken Englishman to spark a revival in Swiss international football. Roy Hodgson, a former non-league player in England, became coach to Switzerland's national squad in 1993 after serving with a number of South African, Swedish and Swiss clubs.

Hodgson took Switzerland to the '94 World Cup finals in the USA, for the first time in twenty-eight years. They reached the Second Round before losing 3-0 to Spain.

Now Roy has worked some more of his magic, this time reaching the European Championship finals in England. His team finished top of Qualifying Group 3, ahead of Turkey, Sweden, Hungary and Iceland.

The coach's obvious talents caught the eye of Italian giants Inter Milan, and he became their coach in the autumn of 1995. A few months afterwards he was replaced as Swiss coach by Artur Jorge who will want to carry on Roy's good work.

Marco Grassi jumps for the ball

THE ROAD TO ENGLAND QUALIFYING GROUP THREE

Iceland	0	Sweden	1
Hungary	2	Turkey	2
Turkey	5	Iceland	0
Switzerland	**4**	**Sweden**	**2**
Switzerland	**1**	**Iceland**	**0**
Sweden	2	Hungary	0
Turkey	**1**	**Switzerland**	**2**
Turkey	2	Sweden	1
Hungary	**2**	**Switzerland**	**2**
Hungary	1	Sweden	0
Switzerland	**1**	**Turkey**	**2**
Sweden	1	Iceland	1
Iceland	2	Hungary	1
Iceland	**0**	**Switzerland**	**2**
Sweden	**0**	**Switzerland**	**0**
Turkey	2	Hungary	0
Switzerland	**3**	**Hungary**	**0**
Iceland	0	Turkey	0
Hungary	1	Iceland	0
Sweden	2	Turkey	2

	P	W	D	L	F	A	Pts
Switzerland	8	5	2	1	15	7	17
Turkey	8	4	3	1	16	8	15
Sweden	8	2	3	3	9	10	9
Hungary	8	2	2	4	7	13	8
Iceland	8	1	2	5	3	12	5

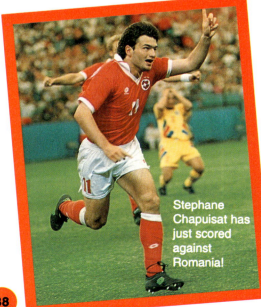

Stephane Chapuisat has just scored against Romania!

FACT FILE
GOVERNING BODY: Schweizerischer Fussballverband, Berne
FOUNDED: 1895
NATIONAL COLOURS: Red shirts, white shorts, red socks
MANAGER/COACH: Artur Jorge
PREVIOUS BEST IN EUROPEAN CHAMPIONSHIP: First Round in 1964

TURKEY

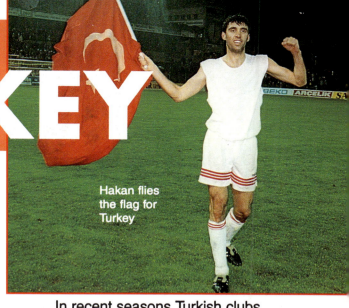

Hakan flies the flag for Turkey

THE ROAD TO ENGLAND
QUALIFYING GROUP THREE

Iceland	0	Sweden	1
Hungary	**2**	**Turkey**	**2**
Turkey	**5**	**Iceland**	**0**
Switzerland	4	Sweden	2
Switzerland	1	Iceland	0
Sweden	2	Hungary	0
Turkey	**1**	**Switzerland**	**2**
Turkey	**2**	**Sweden**	**1**
Hungary	2	Switzerland	2
Hungary	1	Sweden	0
Switzerland	**1**	**Turkey**	**2**
Sweden	1	Iceland	1
Iceland	2	Hungary	1
Icealnd	0	Switzerland	2
Sweden	0	Switzerland	0
Turkey	**2**	**Hungary**	**0**
Switzerland	3	Hungary	0
Iceland	**0**	**Turkey**	**0**
Hungary	1	Iceland	0
Sweden	**2**	**Turkey**	**2**

	P	W	D	L	F	A	Pts
Switzerland	8	5	2	1	15	7	17
Turkey	**8**	**4**	**3**	**1**	**16**	**8**	**15**
Sweden	8	2	3	3	9	10	9
Hungary	8	2	2	4	7	13	8
Iceland	8	1	2	5	3	12	5

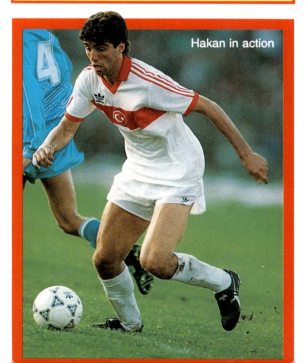

Hakan in action

In recent seasons Turkish clubs, like Trabzonspor, Besiktas, Fenerbache and Galatasary have become prominent in Europe – just ask Manchester United for confirmation of that regarding Galatasary!

Now the Turkish national side, under brilliant coach and former international player Fatih Terim, has made it to the 1996 European Championship finals by finishing as runners-up to Switzerland in Qualifying Group 3. And they did it in some style, recording some fine victories along the way. The clincher, though, was a 2-2 draw with Sweden in the last game. It was a result which saw the unexpected elimination of the Swedes who staged the last Championship final four years ago.

Turkey are captained by the country's appearance record holder Oguz Cetin, but their real danger man is striker Hakan Suker, known as 'The Bull'. Despite his apparent failure with Torino in the Italian League and his subsequent return to his former club Galatasary, you can bet Hakan 'The Bull' will pose a real threat this summer.

FACT FILE
GOVERNING BODY: Federation Turque De Football, Ankara
FOUNDED: 1923
NATIONAL COLOURS: White shorts, white shorts, red socks
MANAGER/COACH: Fatih Terim
PREVIOUS BEST IN EUROPEAN CHAMPIONSHIP: First Round in 1960 and 1964

THE STORY EUROPEAN

1960

The idea for a championship of European football was originally suggested by Henri Delaunay the secretary of FIFA as long ago as 1927. But the idea was not taken seriously until after the formation of UEFA in 1954.

Sadly M. Delaunay died in 1955, before his dream - initially called the European Nations' Cup - became a reality.

The first qualifying tournament began in 1958, with the finals staged two years later in Delaunay's home country, France. The trophy was named the Henri Delaunay Cup, in his honour.

Amazingly only seventeen nations applied to contest the tournament, among the absentees were the four home nations of Great Britain and West Germany.

Eventually only Yugoslavia and the USSR remained in the tournament. They played the first European Nations final at the Parc des Princes stadium, in Paris, on 10 July 1960.

Yugoslavia attacked right from the start and the great Russian goalkeeper Lev Yashin had to be at the top of his game, but even he could not prevent Galic scoring for Yugoslavia in the 40th minute.

In the second half the USSR staged a revival. Within five minutes of the restart they equalised through winger Metreveli. The score remained at 1-1 after 90 minutes, and the match went into extra time. In the end the stamina of the Russians decided the matter and Ponedelnik scored the winning goal for them after 113 minutes of play.

EUROPEAN NATIONS' CUP FINAL
10 July 1960
Parc des Princes, Paris
Attendance 17,966
USSR 2, YUGOSLAVIA 1 (after extra time)

1964

Twenty-nine countries took part in the second European Nations' Cup. This time England, Wales and Northern Ireland were included (but not Scotland). However, by the time of the finals, held in Spain, none of the three British entrants remained in contention. The final, between Spain and the USSR, was played in Madrid, in front of 120,000 fans. They saw a rather dull game in which Spain took the lead on 6 minutes, through Pereda. A minute later the USSR were level thanks to a soft goal by Khusainov.

The winner came in the 84th minute - a spectacular diving header from Spain's Marcellino.

EUROPEAN NATIONS' CUP FINAL
21 June 1964
Bernabau Stadium, Madrid
Attendance 120,000
SPAIN 2, USSR 1

OF THE CHAMPIONSHIP

1968

In the third series the European Nations' Cup became 'The European Championship', and thirty-two nations took part - including Scotland and West Germany for the first time. Among the favourites for the title were England, the 1966 World Cup winners. In the event they finished third after elimination in the semi-finals by Yugoslavia, and a 2-0 victory over the USSR in the third-place play-off. The final itself, between Yugoslavia and Italy, was played in Rome's Olympic Stadium.

Italy were weakened by injury and Yugoslavia proved the dominant team, going ahead through Dzajic on 40 minutes. In the 81st minute Italy equalised from a hotly-disputed free-kick taken by Domenghini. The ref, who had been pushing back the defensive wall when the kick was taken, awarded the goal despite the Yugoslav's protests. The scoreline remained at 1-1 after extra time, and the replay took place in Rome two days later.

This time Italy took command with a completely reorganised team. They won 2-0 with goals from Riva and Anastasi. It was the second time a host nation had won the championship.

EUROPEAN CHAMPIONSHIP FINAL
8 June 1968
Olympic Stadium, Rome
Attendance 88,000
ITALY 1, YUGOSLAVIA 1
Replay - 10 June
ITALY 2, YUGOSLAVIA 0

1972

The 1972 finals were staged in Belgium and for the third time the USSR reached the final. Their opponents were West Germany who had arrived via a quarter-final defeat of England and a semi-final defeat of the host nation.

The final was played in Brussels, and the magical combination of Beckenbauer, Netzer and Muller proved too much for the Russians. Muller scored twice and Wimmer once for a 3-0 scoreline.

The West German side were now unquestionably masters of European football (two years later they would win the World Cup final, beating Holland in Munich).

EUROPEAN CHAMPIONSHIP FINAL
18 June 1972
Heysel Stadium, Brussels
Attendance 43,437
WEST GERMANY 3, USSR 0

1976

The 1976 finals took place in Yugoslavia, and were the finest and most exciting to date.

England, Scotland and Northern Ireland all failed to qualify for the final stages, but Wales did, eventually reaching the quarter-finals before going out at the hands of Yugoslavia. The host nation went out in the semi-finals after defeat by West Germany.

In the other semi-final Holland's team of superstars, led by Johan Cruyff, lost out to Czechoslovakia.

The Czechoslovakia v West Germany final was played in Belgrade and it proved to be a classic. Czechoslovakia scored first through Svehlic, who netted at the second attempt after the German keeper failed to clear his initial effort.

Then Franz Beckenbauer making his 100th international appearance failed to clear a free-kick and Dobias hit home the Czech's second goal. Shortly before half-time Muller pulled one back for Germany, heading home a cross from Bonhof.

In the second half Czechoslovakia grew tired, and eventually the relentless German pressure paid off with an equaliser headed home by Holzenbein. The game went into extra time, but the scoreline remained at 2-2.

For the first time the European Championship was decided by a penalty shoot-out. The stalemate was broken when Germany's Hoeness missed. Then Panenka chipped the ball over Meier and into the net for Czechoslovakia's hard-earned victory.

EUROPEAN CHAMPIONSHIP FINAL
20 June 1976
Belgrade
Attendance 45,000
CZECHOSLOVAKIA 2, WEST GERMANY 2 (aet)
(Czechoslovakia won on penalties)

1980

The 1980 tournament saw a change in the structure of the finals. This time the championship would be decided via a two group system split among the eight qualifying nations. The group winners would meet in the final. The group runners-up would play-off for third place.

For the first time the host nation was chosen in advance and would receive automatic entry to the final stages, as in the World Cup. The first country chosen was Italy.

The final was eventually contested in Rome by West Germany and Belgium. The dominant Germans went close in the fourth minute with only a finger-tip save from Pfaff denying Muller. Six minutes later, Schuster played a delicate one-two with Allofs and then floated the ball into the path of Hrubesch who hit the opening goal. The second half saw an injury to Germany's Briegel who had been the best player in the match. His substitution by Cullmann, seemed to upset West Germany's balance, and Belgium began to get back into the game. In the 71st minute Van Der Eycken equalised from the penalty-spot after Van Der Elst had been brought down by Stielike.

Then in the last minute of normal time, and with the match poised to go into extra time, Hrubesch notched the winner from a Rumminigge corner.

French players receive the trophy after their European Championship final victory over Spain in 1984

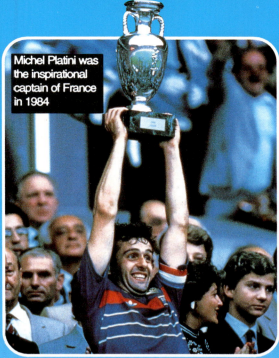

Michel Platini was the inspirational captain of France in 1984

West Germany had won their second European Championship.

EUROPEAN CHAMPIONSHIP FINAL
22 June 1980
Olympic Stadium, Rome
Attendance 47,864
WEST GERMANY 2, BELGIUM 1

1984

France hosted the 1984 European Championship finals and they dominated the tournament under the inspiration of their brilliant skipper, and European Footballer of the Year, Michel Platini.

The France v Portugal semi-final, played in Lyon, is still remembered as one of the best matches in European Championship history. Full of style, passion and excitement it went into extra time with France eventually winning 2-1.

In the final the hosts met Spain in another classic encounter. Both teams had gone close in the first half, but neither had scored. The deadlock was broken eleven minutes into the second half, when Platini curled a free-kick around the Spanish wall and into Arconada's goal.

Le Roux was sent off with six minutes to go, but despite applying much pressure Spain could not take advantage of the situation. In the 90th minute a Spanish attack was halted by a huge clearance by Tigana. The ball reached Bellone, unmarked in the Spanish half. He chipped the ball over Arconada to put the result beyond doubt.

Platini was the man-of-the-match, and the man-of-the-tournament. He had scored in every round and had notched a competition record nine goals.

EUROPEAN CHAMPIONSHIP FINAL
27 June 1984
Parc des Princes Stadium, Paris
Attendance 47,368
FRANCE 2, SPAIN 0

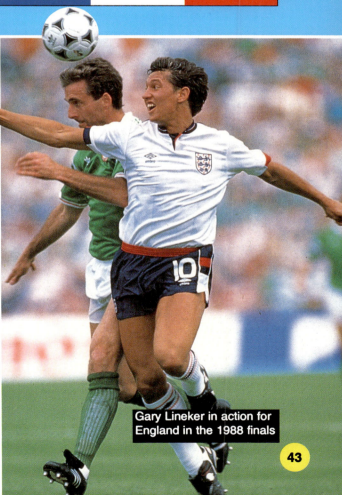

Gary Lineker in action for England in the 1988 finals

1988

The 1988 European Championship finals were held in West Germany. The strongly-fancied host nation reached the semi-finals, but were beaten 2-1 by Holland. In the other semi-final the USSR knocked Italy out of the competition and reached their fourth European Championship final.

The final itself was a great game, with plenty of end-to-end play. Both sides went close early on. Then, in the 33rd minute, Dutch captain Ruud Gullit headed the first goal of the game.

Early in the second half, with the USSR pressing for an equaliser, Holland were forced into some determined defending. But in the 54th minute their troubles were over. A brilliant move involving Van Tiggelen and Muhren was finished off by superstriker Marco van Basten to give the Dutch side a 2-0 cushion which they protected for the remainder of the game.

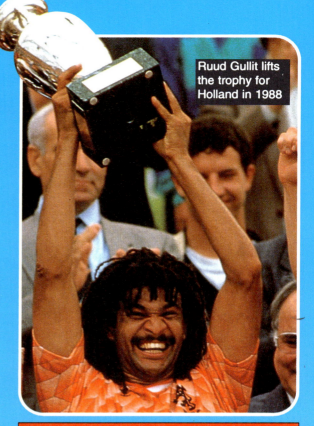

Ruud Gullit lifts the trophy for Holland in 1988

EUROPEAN CHAMPIONSHIP FINAL
25 June 1988
Olympic Stadium, Munich
Attendance 72,308
HOLLAND 2, USSR 0

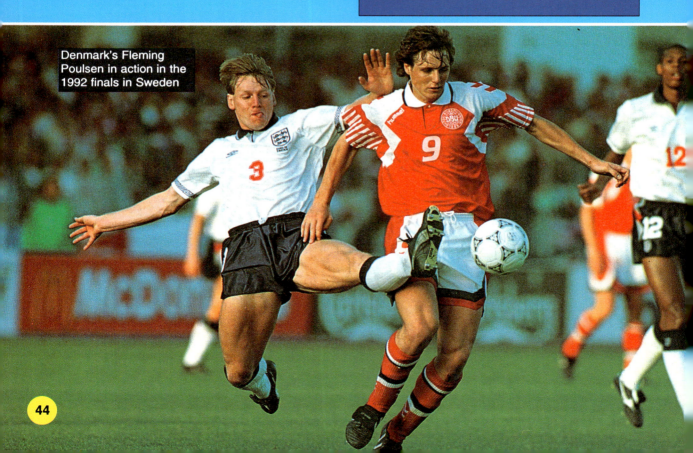

Denmark's Fleming Poulsen in action in the 1992 finals in Sweden

1992

The 1992 finals staged in Sweden told the most dramatic tale in the whole history of the tournament so far. Shortly before the finals were due to begin, Yugoslavia were forced to withdraw because of political unrest. Their place in the finals was taken by Denmark who had finished one point behind Yugoslavia in their qualifying group.

At the eleventh hour, Denmark arrived in Sweden as the tournament's rank outsiders. They were not given a hope of progressing beyond the First Round, let alone winning the title! After all, reasoned the experts, Denmark were unprepared; they had not had time to ready themselves for the task ahead.

But, under the management of Richard Moeller-Nielsen, Denmark chipped their way through to the final where they met mighty Germany, the reigning World Champions no less. Surely, chorused the experts, the Danes must come unstuck this time. Not!

In fact, Denmark proceeded to give Germany a footballing lesson. Within 18 minutes they went ahead when John Jensen powered a shot beyond Bodo Illgner's reach. Then they soaked up all the German pressure and clung on to their slender lead.

In the 78th minute it was all over, thanks to a second Danish goal, scored by Kim Vilfort. Denmark had confounded the critics and were the new Champions of Europe!

Action from the Denmark v Germany final in 1992

EUROPEAN CHAMPIONSHIP FINAL
26 June 1992
Ullevi Stadium, Gothenburg
Attendance 37,800
DENMARK 2, GERMANY 0

Denmark defied the odds to win the European Championship in 1992